CHOOSING TO Love

Hannah Martin

Choosing to Love
© 2017 Hannah Martin
published December 2017

ISBN: 978-0-9997652-0-3

Unless otherwise noted, Scripture quotations taken from The Holy Bible, NIV. Copyright 1973, 1978, 1984, 2011 by Biblica Inc. used by permission. All rights reserved worldwide.

Contact the publisher and/or author at: shmartin06@gmail.com

Cover Art: Rebecca Twardowski:facebook.com/TheSteepedGinger/

Layout and Editing. Publishing Coaching, and project management by: Alane Pearce, Professional Writing Services, LLC. Contact at MyPublishingCoach.com or alane@MyPublishingCoach.com

Dedication

This book is dedicated to my husband, Stephen. You
never gave up on us, you chose to love me even at my worst,
even when I said I was done. You kept pursuing me, you
kept showing me Christ's love. I am forever grateful to your
dedication to me and our family. I love you more than you could
ever know!
-Your Wife

I would also like to dedicate this book to Alane Pearce, for
giving me the courage and encouragement to write it. Thank you
for all of your time, counsel and help with this project! You are
such a gift and a blessing to me!

- Hannah

Introduction

September 2010, we were five years into our marriage. I threw my bags in the trunk and buckled my babies in the back seat. The rain poured all around the car leaving me soaking wet.

"I'm leaving. I can't stay with him anymore. I have completely fallen out of love with him. I hate him."

As I saw his shadow staring at me in the rear view mirror I started to think about our past. I was 16 and he was 18 the first time we met each other. He was charming, kind and had a smile that made my knees go weak. We couldn't get enough of each other. But now all I wanted to do was get away from him.

How had this happened? How had we gotten to this point? How could our once strong, forever love grown so cold?

Life had happened to us.

Five years and two kids later we were struggling. It was hard, and painful, and I didn't want to do this anymore. Disappointments, struggles, empty promises, and unmet expectations had become the norm.

Love wasn't supposed to be this hard; it was supposed to be easy right?

Wasn't this supposed to be a fairy tale?

Wasn't love all we needed?

Weren't we supposed to live happily ever after?!

Choosing to love again was a process. A long, hard, but necessary process. I had to be honest with myself about my broken, because, like my friend Alane Pearce says, "If we never talk about our broken we will never overcome it."

That is what is both beautiful and painful about the process—bringing our broken to the light and letting God expose it and redeem it. We have to get it out, we have to write and talk it through so that we can grow and move forward. Just like a seed planted in the ground, you can choose to believe that the weight is too much, that it's too hard to grow and breakthrough and stay buried and alone. Or you can choose to grow, push through the dirt and reach towards the light until you break through the ground and become something new, something better, something God created and intended for you to be. You are not being buried; you are being planted, if you choose to grow. My hope and prayer for you is that you choose to grow, that you push through and fight because you are worth it.

Your marriage is worth it.

You can do this.

You can choose to love.

What you are about to read is my heart change. This 21-day devotional will walk you through the steps I took to not only love my husband again, but to completely change my relationship with God.

Our marriage is so much stronger than I ever could have hoped or dreamed for. I would do these steps over and over until they became a habit.

Stick with it! God will not disappoint you! He is faithful, and He will see you through. Fix your eyes on Him and be open to what He wants to do in you and in your marriage.

"Now all glory to God, who is able, through his mighty power at work within us, to accomplish infinitely more than we might ask or think." Ephesians 3:20

ℰ

Step One: Write it out

The battles are won in the mind.

What we think leads to what we do. Just like a pot of soup, we put ideas and thoughts into our mind and we let them sit and stew until they become truth in our minds and then we end up acting on those truths. So what do we do with all these thoughts? Get them out! You do that by writing them out. Good or bad, write out your thoughts. Having them in your head is one thing, but seeing them in word form is another. It will help you to see on paper what consumes your mind.

Use the pages in this journal to get your thoughts out!

"...take EVERY thought captive to obey Christ."
2 Corinthians 10:5

Going deeper day one

What kind of thoughts are you having towards your husband right now? Why?

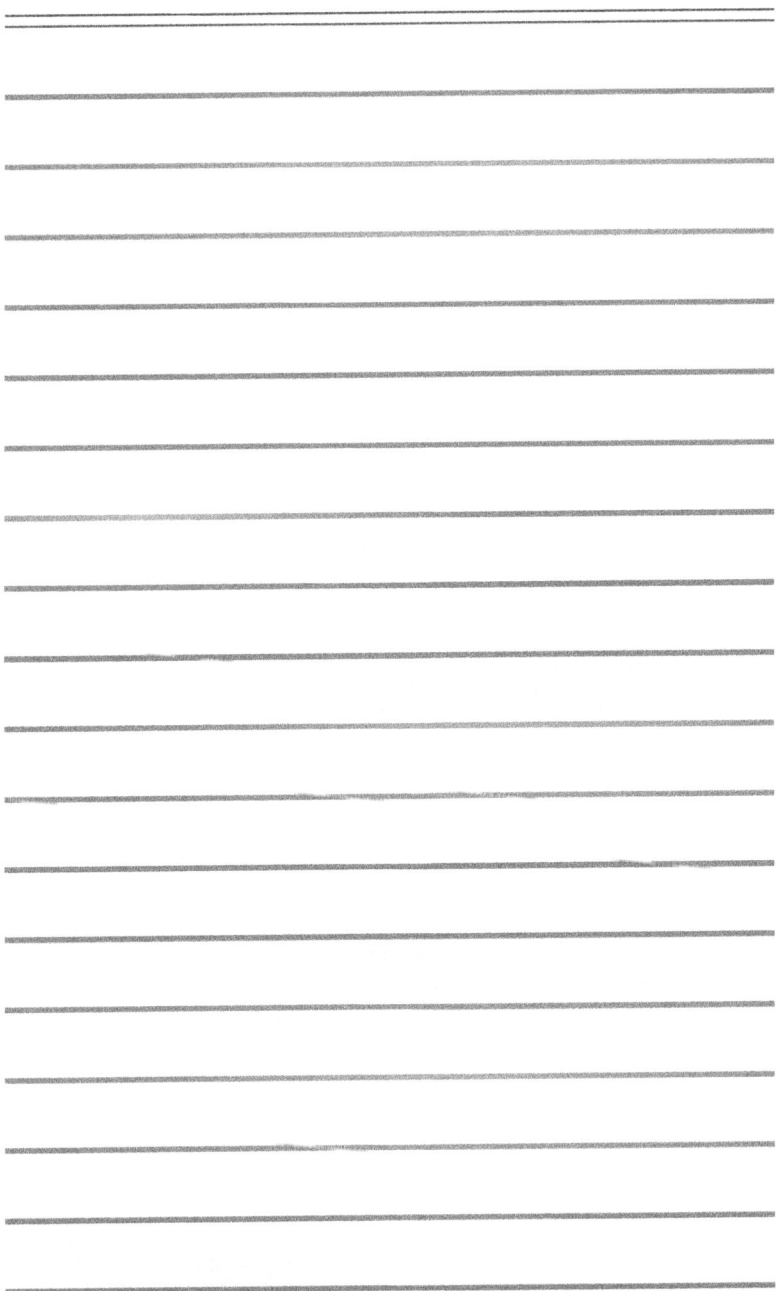

Never underestimate the importance of journaling.

I heard a preacher say one time that, "Satan quivers when our pen touches the paper." Think about what a shame it would be if the disciples never journaled. Imagine not being able to read about Jesus' life here on Earth and what He did for us. Think about all the lives that would never have been changed by the power of the disciples' testimonies. The world is different simply because they decided to write it down.

When we put to paper our story and the process that it took to get through trials, we are putting together our testimony. We are writing the testimony of what God has done and is doing in our lives. It will change people because that is how powerful words and stories are. You have a story, we all do and we were told to share those stories.

"Let the redeemed of the Lord Tell their story."
Psalm 107:2

Going deeper day two

If you could tell your husband how you feel, what would you say?

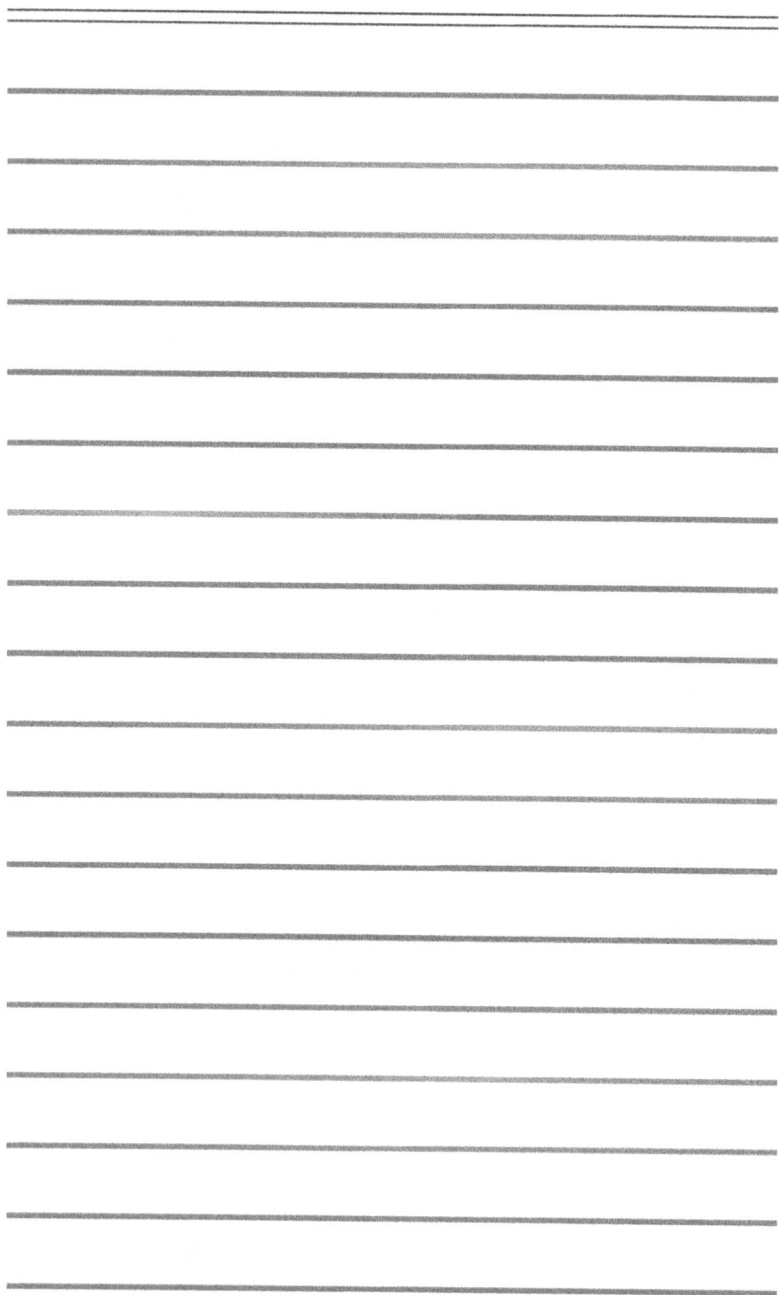

We dated for two years; we played in a youth band together. He was the lead singer and guitarist; I played the keys and sang harmonies. We were smitten with each other. We saw each other every day after school and work. We would sit on my parents' front swing and talk about anything and everything. We talked about getting married someday, buying a house and having kids, but it always seemed like that would be way down the road.

At 17, I found out I was pregnant. That wasn't in the plan, but God has a way of doing things that usually don't align with our plans. I remember the look on Stephen's face when I told him; complete shock and terror. Suddenly he felt the weight of real adult responsibility on his shoulders and it was heavy. How are we going to do this? How are we going to afford a place to live and raise a child? Were we ready?

"Was I ready? Do I really love Stephen enough to get married right now? Or am I forced to marry him because I am pregnant?" These were the doubts and questions that plagued my mind constantly. I loved him, but all of a sudden it seemed like I had to choose to love him forever.

We got married two months later on the rainiest day of the year, October 8th, 2005. Friends and family watched as we said our vows and committed to only love each other for the rest of our lives.

We spent our honeymoon in Gettysburg, PA and stayed in a bed and breakfast that had big gaps under the doors and floors that creaked whenever someone would walk by. You could hear people talking through the paper-thin walls (super romantic). Breakfast was at 7 a.m., and that seemed like dawn to us newlyweds.

We headed home to start our new life as a married couple with a baby due in only 5 short months, and only $7 in our bank account.

Reality was about to hit us hard.

Going deeper day three

If you could sit with God and tell him how you feel, what would you say?

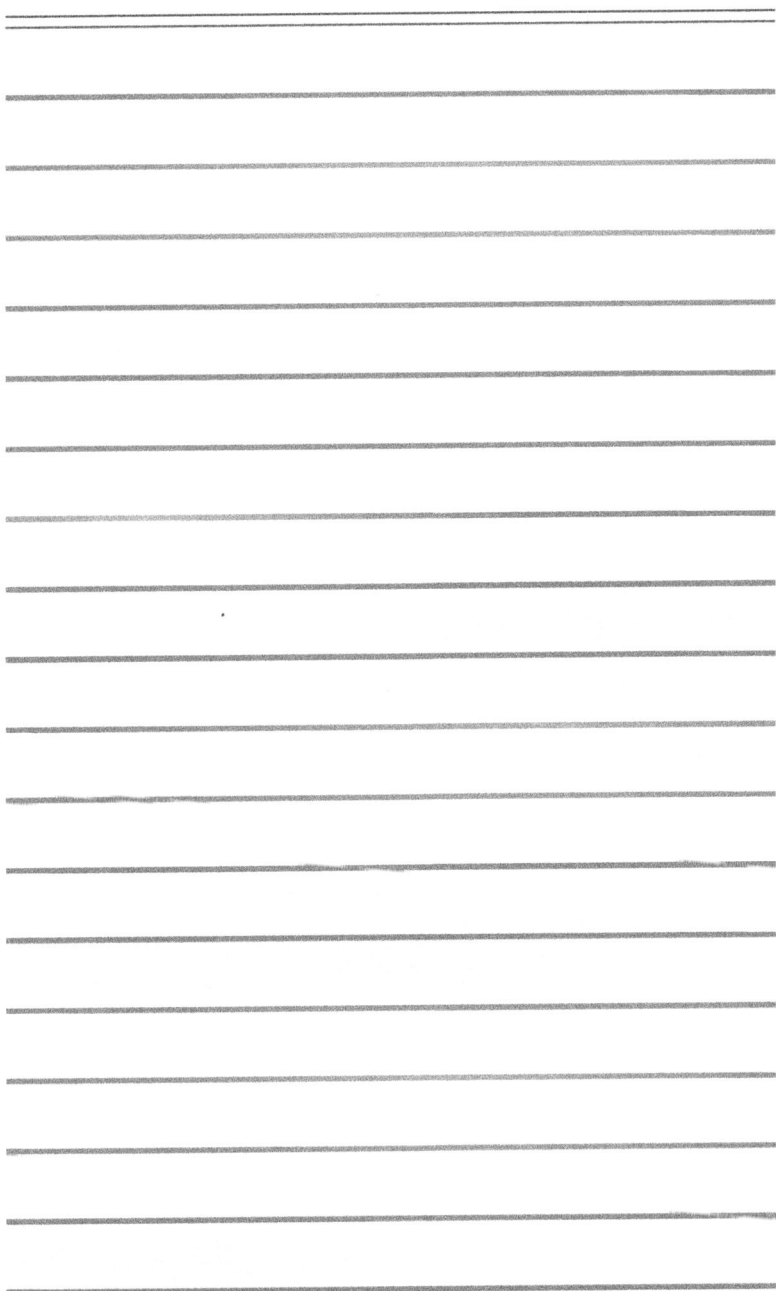

Additional Notes

Step Two: Say it

"Today I will be a faithful wife."

I had to say this to myself every morning. One day at a time. *Today I will show love, today I will be kind, today I will try.*

Even when you don't feel like it, say these words out loud to yourself. Start to cement them into your thinking. When the lies creep into your mind, combat them with truth. Sometimes we need to declare statements until they start to become actions in our life. Words are powerful. God spoke the words and the world was formed, air and space, light and life, creatures and plants, all came into existence because of words.

Anything that is worth it takes time. Anything that is of value doesn't just happen. You need to wage war against the enemy. You need to see this as a battle that Satan isn't going to win. You need to take a stand for your marriage!

It is WORTH FIGHTING FOR!

"Those who plant in tears will reap a harvest with shouts of joy." Psalm 126:5

That is what this season is for you my friend, just like it was for me. A season of planting in tears. Planting in the pain of, "I don't want to, I don't feel like it!" So that you can reap a harvest with shouts of joy! Think about your children (if you have them). Think about the legacy you will leave for them. A family, together–not torn apart. Not another victim of divorce and heartbreak. In this broken world...be different. Our marriages directly reflect the relationship between Christ and the church (His people). We should be different. We should have marriages and relationships that are attractive, vulnerable and hopeful. God stopped at nothing to save us, to mend what was broken, to get us back. We need to have the same fight and passion for our spouse and our marriage.

Going deeper day four

What was your parent's relationship like? How do you think their example of relationship has affected your relationship with your husband?

December 2006, our son was 9 months old at the time, the apartment we were living in had black mold and it was making him sick. We had to move, but we were so poor, and all of the apartments in our area were way more than we could afford. So we moved into a basement apartment of a family friend who'd we'd known for many years.

There was a single, young man who lived above us with his parents. He was a good friend of ours, who once had a crush on me back when I was in middle and high school, that should have been a warning sign, but I ignored it. My husband worked long days and when he came home in the evenings he would "check out". He didn't want to help with the baby or housework; the TV claimed his time and attention just about every night. I was studying to be a Certified Nursing Assistant and was working at a local hospital to bring in extra money. I was lonely and tired, and the man upstairs noticed.

He got home from his job in the early afternoon. He would come down and visit with me and my son, he offered to watch him so I could study; he offered to drive me to work, pick me up, and even bring me lunch on Saturdays when I worked a full day. It was then that I stopped seeking my husband's attention and sought his attention instead.

I found myself looking forward to time alone with him, I would sit outside and wait for him to come home. I would have long talks about my husband, my marriage, and my feelings with him. Letting my mind and thoughts wander and go places it shouldn't. Letting my mind daydream about a life I could have with him instead of my husband. I let those thoughts completely take over and I started acting on those thoughts. I threw caution to the wind, ignored what I knew was right and gave in to what I thought would make me happy.

Going deeper day five

What are some of the choices that you made that have made in hopes that it would make you happy?

Happy.

Such a dangerous word.

We cling to this word and use it as a right to pursue anyone or anything. We use it to justify our selfish actions and desires. "You deserve to be happy" is one of the world's greatest lies. Satan sows this lie down in the deepest part of our hearts and uses it to put a wedge between us and our Creator.

Something I learned that completely changed my life is that God is not concerned with our happiness...He's concerned with our holiness.

Did you get that?!

Crazy, I know!

Just let that thought sink in for a minute. He will use people, situations and any means necessary to reach you. He cares so much about drawing you to himself and transforming you into someone who looks more like Him, that He will allow you to get to the place where you are standing on the brink of disaster and you have two choices...live for yourself or live for Him?

WHO are you striving after? Yourself or God?

I was only concerned about me, what I thought would make me happy. I had a plan for the rest of my life and I could make my own dreams come true. But it was quite the opposite; it was the darkest, loneliest and saddest place I had ever experienced.

Going deeper day six

Be honest with yourself. What are you striving after...happiness or holiness?

Additional Notes

Step Three: **Pray it**

Get on your knees and beg God for this.

Beg Him for the feelings again.

Beg Him to speak to you through His word.

Beg Him to bring healing to your marriage.

Beg Him for the strength, love and courage to succeed in your marriage.

Beg Him for the heart, and attitude of Christ.

Beg Him for a desire for your husband again.

Prayer is our most powerful and most underutilized weapon we have. We have direct access to the throne of God himself but we rarely use it. He is waiting to help you, He is waiting to jump in and rescue you, He is longing to lavish his promises on you, but you have to ask for it.

You have to want it.

Going deeper day seven

Have you ever experienced a time when prayer changed a situation or circumstance?

"You can ask for anything in my name, and I will do it, so that the Son can bring glory to the Father. Yes, ask me for anything in my name, and I will do it!" John 14:13-14

I love the second part of John 14:13-14. Jesus knew our little minds would second guess Him, He had to reiterate the point He was making. "Yes, for real! Ask for anything IN MY NAME..."

The problem is that we ask for things in our name. We ask for what we want, what will line up with our plans and our desires, instead of seeking His plan, His desires and what He wants for us.

We have direct access to the throne of God, the Creator of all things, but we rarely use it. We discount its power and so God waits, He waits for us to want it.

Is there anything that is too hard for Him?

Restoring and redeeming things that are beyond our understanding and control are His specialty!

He enjoys reclaiming and repairing everything and anything that is broken. It is impossible to be in the presence of God and not be changed.

I used to say, "Well I just don't feel close to God anymore," and while that may have been true, God was not the one who moved. Every step that I made towards what I thought would make me happy was a step away from a God who truly loved and cared about me. I was chasing "happiness" but I was the saddest I had ever been. It was the loneliest, most depressing years of my life, because I was running away from the real true source of Joy.

Going deeper day eight

Do you think that pain is necessary for growth? Why?

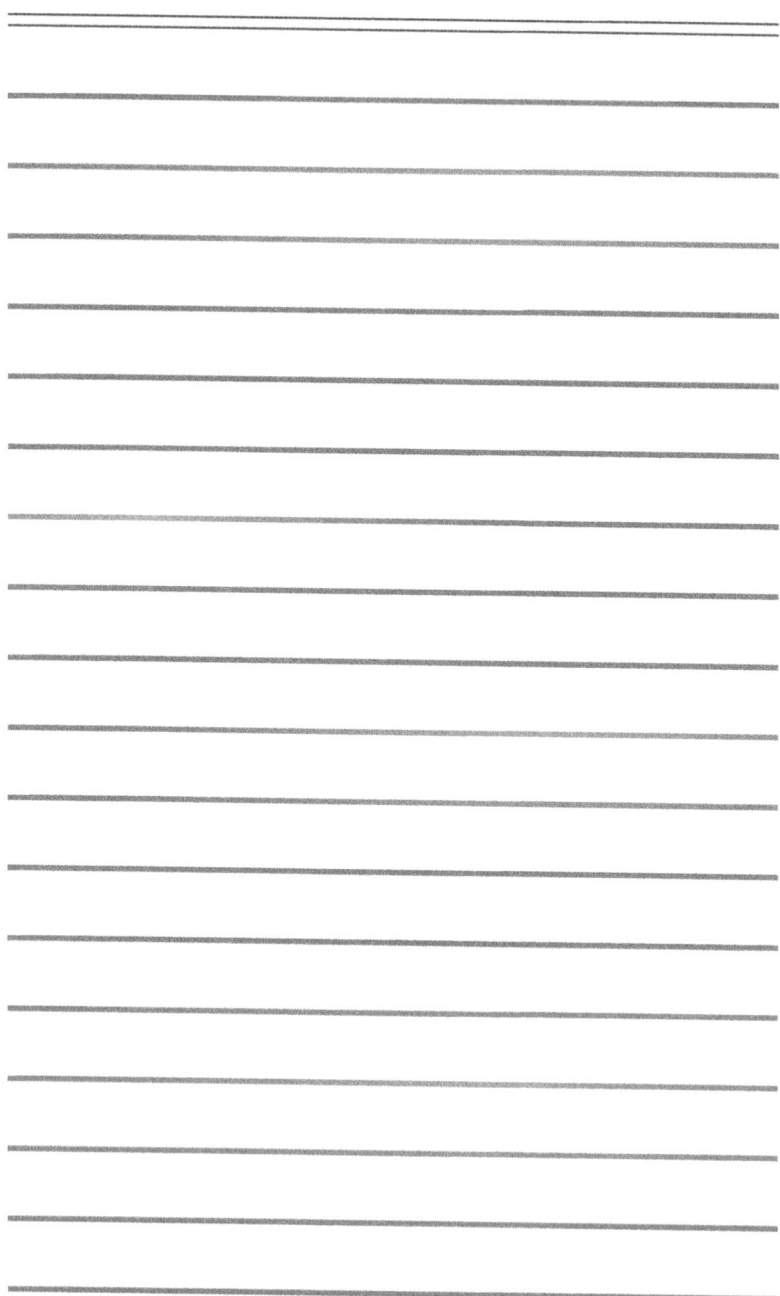

Three years.

That's how long my emotional affair with the other man went on. Three long, excruciating, painful years. I had torn my husband's heart apart; I had destroyed his self-confidence and left him a shattered, insecure man. I had made our home no longer a home. Instead it was a fragile, sad, lonely place where love no longer was evident.

I did that, and I felt nothing. I was hollow and cold inside. I had shut just about everyone out of my life. I smiled and acted the role of happy mom to my kids but they could see right thru it. Many times I considered ending my life. I thought maybe if I just gave up and ended it that my kids, my friends and the world would be better off without me. This is the power of sin. When we let it lead our choices, actions and feelings we let it drive us down the darkest deepest path. We question our worth, value and even the reason we were created. But the scariest thing was that I had become comfortable with my sin. I had become so comfortable that I was willing to take advantage of Christ's sacrifice on the cross. I was willing to say, "It's okay, I know God will forgive me."

I loved myself and my dream for my life more than I loved God and His plan for my life. What a scary place to be. It's like I was standing before Jesus while He was hanging on the cross and seeing Him suffering in pain, slowly dying, and me spitting on Him. Spitting on His act of perfect love for me, and I refused it.

See, that's what it all comes down to, who do you love more?

That was the question I had to answer, that was the troubling thing for me. Was I willing to stand before God and justify myself for breaking the covenant I made with my husband? I was torn between my flesh and my soul.

Satan thought he had me, and he almost did.

Going deeper day nine

When you look at the choices you have made, who do you love more? Yourself or God?

Additional Notes

Step Four: Read it

Get yourself in the word!

Saturate your mind and heart in His promises, in His power. We ask God for His guidance and we ask Him to speak to us but then we don't look where He has already written it out for us.

He wants to speak to you, personally and intentionally. He wants to pour out His wisdom and love on you, but you have to be willing to read His letter to you. You have to open His word and let it sink down deep. I needed His word. I needed to saturate my mind and heart every morning before I started the day because I was so far from God.

Every time I opened the Bible I was drawing closer to God, I could feel Him drawing me back, pulling me in, letting me know He was with me; He was with me in the whole time. Waiting for me to turn around and come back to Him.

Don't stop reading daily, even if you don't feel Him, or get anything out of it. Keep reading, keep pursuing Him. He is faithful, He will speak to you, He will guide you and lead you.

You are not alone.

You never have been.

He is with you.

"For the word of God is living and active, sharper than any two-edged sword, piercing to the division of soul and of spirit, of joints and of marrow, and discerning the thoughts and intentions of the heart." Hebrews 4:12

Going deeper day ten

Are you letting His word expose your dark, ugly places? What are those places?

Are you really giving His word the opportunity to be living and active in your life?

Are you letting the word cut deeper and judge the intentions of your heart?

Are you willing to let it shine a light on all the dark ugly places where we keep our stuff that we don't want to deal with?

I wasn't, and I wasn't going to go far in my marriage until I did.

It wasn't until I started really digging into the word daily, that I began to feel my attitude change. I had to not only read it, but also apply it.

I had to not only read it, but also let it change me. Because girl, it has the power to do that, to ACTUALLY change us from the inside out. It is our light through the darkness of this world. It speaks the truth when all around us are lies. It is our path to life in the Father's presence, the path to true joy. It is our map when we are lost, our voice of reason when we feel insane. It is our comfort when we feel abandoned.

Use it.

Use it to guide you through the darkness of this broken world.

Use it as your pathway to the Father.

"Your word is a lamp unto my feet and a light unto my path." Psalm 119: 106

Going deeper day eleven

Find one scripture right now that you can cling to, what is it? Why?

November 1st, 2010, I was sitting on the park bench, watching my kids play at the park. I had been living at my parent's house for two months. I had moved out of the home my husband and I bought together because I wasn't in love with him anymore. I was a lonely, sad mess because I had chased happiness.

I remember it like it was yesterday. A breeze blew by the left side of my face and I heard a still, low voice say, *"Go Home."* I knew it was God, He was commanding me to do something that I had set my mind against doing.

"But I don't want to!" I said back. "It's too hard, and I don't love him anymore."

The question God asked next was the turning point in not only my marriage but also my life. *"Who are you going to live for?"*

Pastor Drew Shofner once said, "The will of God will always offend the mind." And it was. It was offending me and my plan for Happiness. It was offending all the choices I had made up until this moment.

I sat there in silence, my heart at war with my mind. My flesh was screaming to run. My soul was crying out for its Creator, it longed for the Father. It longed to return home like the prodigal son, I had turned my back on Him and wandered for too long.

I had a choice to make...to live for myself, or to live for God?

I had to decide.

And right then and there on that park bench, the cry of my soul won.

Thank God!

Going deeper day twelve

Are you resisting God's will for your life? If so, how? And why?

Additional Notes

Step Five: See it

Remember when you first fell in love?

The way he looked at you, the way he smiled at you, made you laugh?

Remember the first time he leaned in and kissed you?

The way your stomach would do back flips inside?

Dig down deeper; go way back down memory lane. It's not impossible to feel that again. Feelings can come and go just like the wind but truth is solid, it stands the test of time, and the truth is that once...you did love him and he loved you, otherwise you probably wouldn't have gotten married.

Hold on to that truth!

There is a purpose and a plan for your life and the God who made you, the God who picked your eye color and the shade of your skin, cares about every detail of your life. Nothing is an accident or by chance. You and your husband were joined together for a reason, for a purpose and a plan.

Are you willing to believe that?

Are you willing to work to get the feelings back?

"Dear children, let's not merely say that we love each other; let us show the truth by our actions." 1 John 3:18

Going deeper day thirteen

What first attracted you to your husband? What are some of his good qualities now?

One way to get that feeling back is to notice him again.

See him, look at him, look at him the way you used to. The problem is that you've made a habit out of noticing who he *isn't* and you've missed who HE IS! (I know because I did the same thing.) We see and read fantasies on TV and in books, and we put an unrealistic expectation on our husbands that they will never meet.

We daydream what it would be like to have a perfect husband who is madly in love with us and shows us daily how much we mean to them. We are looking in the wrong place, and we are placing our expectations on the wrong man. The only man who will not fail you loves you more than you could possibly know. He loves you with an extravagant love that carries your sin and shame to a wooden cross and gave his life for you. Jesus, the only man who loved you to death.

You loved your husband for a reason; you married him for a reason. Take a moment to remember and write those things down. Whatever it takes, if you need to look through old photos, videos, read old love letters, listen to those songs that the two of you had together...do it! Relight the flame that has gone out.

Love is a choice not a feeling.

Choose to fall in love again.

"My beloved friends, let us continue to love each other since love comes from God. Everyone who loves is born of God and experiences a relationship with God. The person who refuses to love doesn't know the first thing about God, because God is love—so you can't know him if you don't love."
1 John 4:7-8 (The Message)

Going deeper day fourteen

What are some of the expectations that you put on your husband?

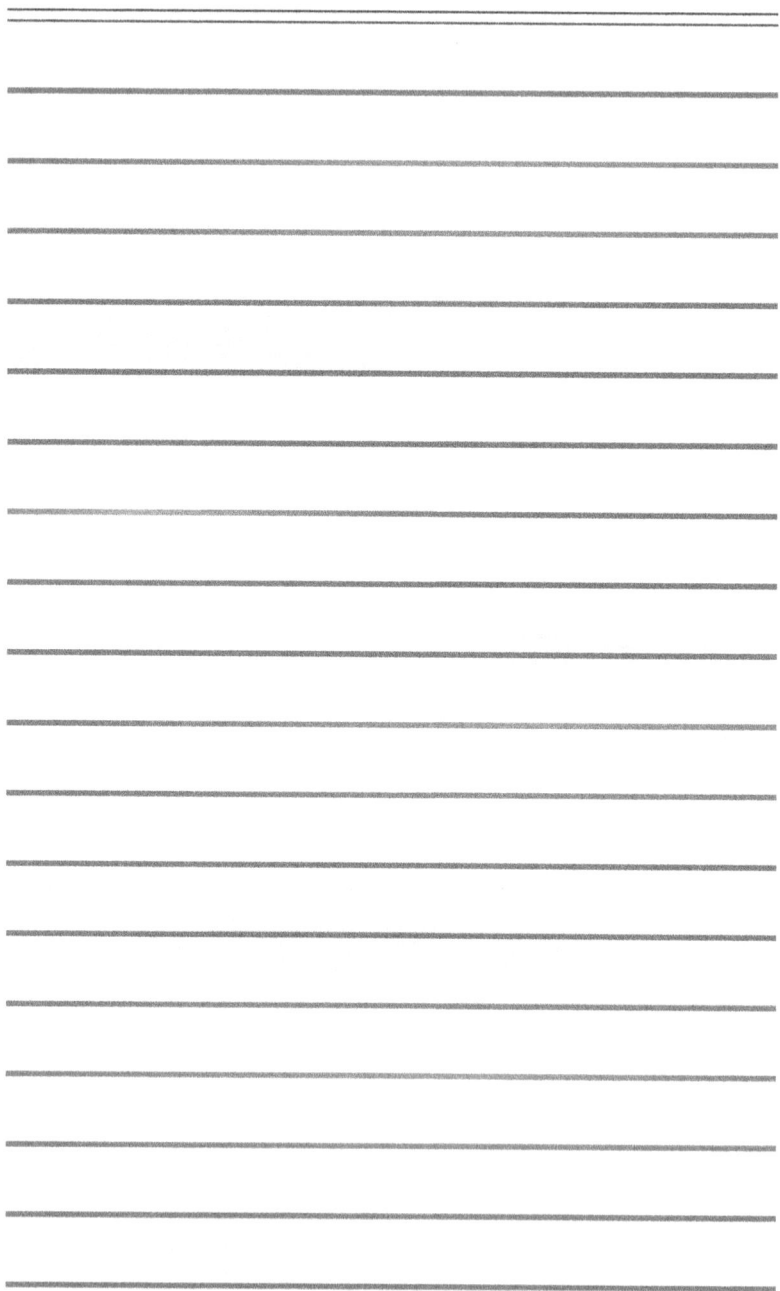

I'd like to say that right after that day on the park bench that my whole life turned around, and my marriage was perfect, and I was happy all the time, and I never had to struggle again...But that is just not the truth.

The truth is that day was the turning point but I now had a long, hard journey ahead of me. Where God was going to put every promise He had for me to the test.

I had the constant choice to surrender my wants and desires to God and trust that He would replace them with His wants and desires. I had hit rock bottom. I didn't know who I was anymore, I didn't have an identity, and I didn't have a solid moral foundation to stand on. I was completely lost in my own darkness.

That's what Satan does. He calls us away from our Father and strips us of our self worth and identity in Christ. Apart from God we are nothing, we have nothing and we are powerless against the darkness. So the darkness consumes us and eats us alive.

It's not until we realize that our only hope, our only chance, our only worth is in Christ alone, that we can stand against the darkness. Jesus overcame all evil the day he breathed new life after the death on the cross. He answered all of our doubts, fears and insecurities on the cross. He said, *you are worth it and I will prove it with my life* when he hung, battered and bloody.

We have nothing apart from Him.

We can overcome nothing without Him.

"In Him was life, and that life was the light of men. The Light shines in the darkness, and the darkness has not overcome it." 1 John 1:4-5

Going deeper day fifteen

What is an insecurity or fear that you struggle with? Do you believe God can help you overcome it?

I went home.

That day at the park changed something in me. I didn't magically fall in love again with my husband, but I was willing to put God's word to the test. I was willing to see if God really had the best plan for my life. So I went back to my parent's house, burned the separation papers that I had filled out and was ready to send in, packed up my clothes and went home.

Home to a fragile man that I had broken.

Back to a shattered marriage that I had destroyed.

Back to my two small children who were feeling the side effects of a shattered Mom and Dad.

And I dragged my feet the whole way.

I was going back with the pieces of what was left in my hands and laid them at the feet of the Healer and simply said, "Fix it. I can't," with tears streaming down my face.

God heard me, and God saw me, and He was so ready and willing to pick up my mess and help us put it back together.

Going deeper day sixteen

Do you want this? Do you really want your marriage to fail?
Do you really want to chase your own idea of happiness?

Step Six: Do it

This one was hard for me because I didn't feel like it, and I didn't want to. But there is a point where we have to move past our feelings and force ourselves to DO the hard work. It WILL change you; it will soften your heart towards him

Do love in action. Put him first--before the kids, before the dishes, before the laundry. Show him that he is still a priority. Write him notes, cook his favorite meal, laugh with him, plan a date Night. Kiss him...with passion! Be happy when he walks in the door, hold his hand in public. Show him that you are trying.

Keep doing it, even if you don't think he notices, even if you think he's not changing. You can't change him. Only God changes people. But you can show him love, and through that love God will use it, He will honor your sacrifice and you will be blessed. Be the spouse you would want to have.

"Be devoted to one another in love. Honor one another above yourselves." Romans 12:10

Slowly we began to heal. God wrapped His grace around us and began to tend to our deeper wounds that we had lashed into one another. Months of counseling, hours of prayer, mornings spent pouring over God's word...We got connected in a good, Bible based church and many "fight fors" later, we began to see the change in our marriage.

There was a shift in my life when I began to live my life asking, "How does God get the glory in this?"

My life stopped revolving around my small plan and turned into something so much bigger...God's plan.

When we submit and say, "You can have it all, all my broken pieces, all my mess, You take it and do with it what You want." God shows up and it's so much more than we could ever have dreamed or imagined.

He collects our shattered pieces of life and turns them into a beautiful piece of art that He proudly displays for His glory, but you have to be willing to surrender them all first.

It's hard to let go, and let Him take control, but that's the only way He can begin to put what we broke, back together again.

Going deeper day seventeen

Where are you finding God's grace in your relationship?

It's not too late!
Your marriage is not too far gone.
He brought the dead back to life, He's got this.
He can restore the most broken things.

I never would've thought that our sad, hot mess of a marriage could be restored, but it has. Only by the grace and glory of God. You have to know and believe that your heavenly Father loves you something fierce! That He longs to make you whole and see you smile with true Joy. Hold on to that truth!

Going deeper day eighteen

Write a prayer to God submitting your life to His bigger and better plan.

Additional Notes

Step Seven: Get a buddy

This one is really important!

You need to be able to confide in someone; you can't keep this all inside. BUT, they need to be FOR your marriage...Do not confide in someone who is just going to tell you what you want to hear.

You need a friend who is going to hold your hand and lead you to the foot of the cross, over and over again.

Someone who is rooted in the word of God and can speak truth into your life.

Someone who will be able to see and hear about your broken and love you through it.

A trustworthy person who will keep your stuff to themselves and not spread it around for everyone to know and judge.

"Make this your common practice: Confess your sins to each other and pray for each other so that you can live together whole and healed." James 5:16 (The Message)

Going deeper day nineteen

What is the truth that God is teaching you about your marriage?

Frannie Miller saw what could be.

She was sent into my life to remind me that God was not done with me yet and that my marriage is worth fighting for. She was an older woman in the church that I grew up in. She knew me since I was a baby.

Her husband, Steve, likes to remind me of a time when he watched me in the nursery; he was holding me in his lap and he heard me chewing on something. He looked down to see what it was and saw bubble gum all over my mouth and his tie! He loves telling that story, and jokes that I owe him a tie.

I grew up playing with their kids. Frannie watched me grow from a child into a teenager, then a wife and then mother. She knew that what I was doing was not what God wanted for me. She would come to my parent's house while I was separated from my husband and ask to take me to coffee.

I dreaded it. And often times I would decline her offer to go, but she kept pursuing me. I knew what she was going to do. She was going to read Bible verses to me that would convict me, hold my hands and pray over me and tell me that I should love my husband.

And guess what. She did those things and more.

She spoke truths over me and reminded me that I had at one time loved my husband. That my life was not about me; that it was meant to glorify God and in doing that I would find true joy.

Slowly God used her words to break through my cold heart and real change started to happen. I couldn't have gotten to the place of real change without her. I am so thankful for her persistence and commitment to me and my marriage.

My friend, you weren't made to do this alone! None of us were. Life is hard. We need each other; we need to pray with and for each other. We need to be willing to cry out to our heavenly Father for each other.

A road is less lonely when you have a trustworthy friend walking with you.

Seek them out, get involved at your church, join a small group,

Bible study, prayer group, or anywhere you can find trustworthy women. You might be surprised at how willing women are to be connected, and that your story may sound a lot like someone else's.

And who knows, someday you might be the one who is telling a lonely, broken woman, "Let me tell you what God did in my marriage; He saved mine, and He can save yours!"

Be brave! Get out there and get connected!

Going deeper day twenty

Who is the buddy God is leading you to speak to about your marriage? If you don't know, write down some ways that you can find such a person to mentor you.

This next verse is one of my favorites. I have it written on a post-it note by my coffee machine to remind me every morning...

"God is within her, she WILL NOT fail.
He will be with her at the break of day."
Psalm 46:5 (emphasis mine)

He WILL BE WITH YOU!

And if He is with you, all things are possible.

I pray that you will know the extravagant love your Heavenly Father has for you. That He is working all things for your good. Use this process to grow and change you, because when we stop growing we die.

Going deeper day twenty one

What are the five things you are most certain about in this journey? How will you use them to help you choose to love again?

_____

_____

_____

_____

_____

_____

_____

_____

_____

_____

_____

_____

_____

_____

_____

_____

_____

_____

_____

You, through the power of Christ, can do this!

All of heaven is cheering you on!

Don't quit, don't give up!

Watch God show up and amaze you.

I promise, you won't regret it.

With love and prayers,
-Hannah

P.S. I have one more assignment for you on the following page. It's time, so don't skip it.

Use the following pages to write a love letter to your spouse. It's time you tell him how much he really means to you and where you want to go from here.

About the Author

    Hannah lives in Ellicott City Maryland, with her husband and three children. She leads worship at her church in Severn, Maryland. She also writes music, songs, short stories, poems and devotionals for her church and womens' events.

www.ingramcontent.com/pod-product-compliance
Lightning Source LLC
LaVergne TN
LVHW051426080426
835508LV00022B/3262